SOMERSIZE DESSERTS

SOMERSIZE
DESSERTS
Suzanne Somers

CROWN
PUBLISHERS
New York

To the three million and more Somersizers, this one's for you!

Copyright © 2001 by Suzanne Somers
Photographs copyright © Jeff Katz

Published by Crown Publishers, New York, New York.
Member of the Crown Publishing Group.

Random House, Inc. New York, Toronto, London, Sydney, Auckland
www.randomhouse.com

CROWN is a trademark and the Crown colophon is a registered trademark of Random House, Inc.

Printed in the United States of America

Design by Lauren Dong

Library of Congress Cataloging-in-Publication Data is available on request.

ISBN 0-609-60977-7

10 9 8 7 6 5 4 3 2 1

First Edition

Contents

The team.

Acknowledgments

This is my fourth book in the Somersize series, and I've had the good fortune to put together an extraordinary team. In particular, my daughter-in-law, Caroline Somers, who is my ace. I really couldn't put out this kind of volume without her. She's smart as a whip and knows more about the Somersize program than anyone.

Denise Vivaldo runs our test kitchen, and she is incredible. Denise understands not only flavor but the chemistry of food as well. With SomerSweet, it was essential to reformulate tried-and-true recipes and compensate for the lack of bulk. Denise and her partner, Andy Sheen-Turner, knew how to do that.

Once again my photographer of choice was Jeff Katz, and he really outdid himself this time. These photographs are so clean and appealing that you can taste and smell the food just by looking at them. Many thanks to Jeff's talented team: Victor Boghossian, Andy Strauss, and Jack Coyier.

My food stylist is the amazing Brian Toffoli, who brought a fresh new look to this project. Many thanks to his assistant, Tish Beckman.

The girls in my office, including Marsha Yanchuck, my longtime assistant and dear friend (who did "dessert research" for me, in particular on Dark Chocolate Mousse). Thanks also to Anka Brazzell, who keeps my crazy schedule in shape, and to Liz Kozakowski.

Many thanks to Jim England.

This is the fourth book with my great editor, Kristin Kiser. She has guided me through the process, overseeing the entire project, and I deeply appreciate her excellence.

Once again, I am grateful for the support of my publishers at Crown: Chip Gibson, Andy Martin, and Steve Ross.

The production team at Crown is first-rate. Many thanks to Mary Schuck for her beautiful cover design, and to Jane Searle, Lauren Dong, Jean Lynch, and Claudia Gabel.

And last but not least, the best literary agent in the business, my pal Al Lowman. This is our sixth together, and who could ask for anything more, except maybe Alan Hamel, my partner in business and in life.

I am extremely grateful to all of you.

SUZANNE SOMERS

Introduction

All my life I have had a sweet tooth. I love cake and sugary frosting and chocolate and pies and pudding and ice cream. I love desserts! Always have and always will. Dessert is an experience to savor. There's just something about the texture of the perfect custard, or the smell of chocolate cake, or the tiny nibble off the crust of a freshly baked pie that fills your mouth and your soul with desire . . . a desire for more!

Dessert is the queen of all courses. It's the coveted finale at the end of the meal. We wait for it. We anticipate the pleasure. We'd go to war over chocolate! All for the passionate, sensual pleasure of eating something rich, delicious, sinful, and forbidden.

As a child I could eat all I wanted and stay as skinny as a rail. My mother would say, "Suzanne, you'd better finish your dinner if you want some dessert." I would tear through the main course to get to the sweets. At the time I didn't have to worry about my weight. My biggest concern about sugar was keeping my teeth brushed. However, as the years went by, those desserts started catching up with me.

Over a decade ago I learned the dangers of sugar and foods high in carbohydrates that turn into sugar upon digestion. That's when my Somersize weight-loss program began. I learned the importance of eliminating sugar from my diet so that I could keep my weight just where I wanted it and gain the benefits of hormonal balance and improved health. But oh, how I missed my sweets! I have tried sugar substitutes, but I don't feel good about eating them and the aftertaste turns me off. Plus, I have found they are virtually impossible to cook with.

In the early days of Somersizing I created a handful of recipes with saccharin for when I absolutely had to have something sweet. It just feels so good to have a dessert when you are on Level One, which is the weight-loss portion of my program.

Once I hit my goal weight and stabilized, I began to maintain my weight on Level Two. On Level Two you may have sugar in moderation. Ahhh! I learned to save up for those sugary treats without my weight fluctuating by more than 5 pounds. But I still didn't get to eat as much dessert as I wanted. I really love my chocolate and my ice cream and my cake. (I am a little pig.) In fact, I am the worst cheater of all when it comes to desserts. So, when I'd overdo it, I'd go back to Level One of my program to get back my balance.

Then my husband received a phone call that changed our lives. The call was from a man who creates products for diabetics. He told Alan that many of his diabetic clients are Somersizing. He had a sugar-free pudding, sweetened with aspartame, that his clients loved, and he was wondering if we wanted to sell it as a Somersize pudding. Alan told him that we did not want to sweeten our products with aspartame. Alan said to him, "If you can find us a product without a lot of chemicals that won't spike your insulin, we'd be very interested."

I thought to myself, "Yeah, sure, Alan. Of course we'd like to make desserts without sugar. Of course we'd like to eat sweets without spiking our insulin level. Who wouldn't? But that's impossible." Well, I was proven wrong. Once again, this breakthrough came from Europe. Could there really be a solution for my sweet tooth? Yes, and I call it SomerSweet.

During the past year we have been through an amazing process of discovering this sweet, incredible product that won't send your insulin levels soaring. We tweaked and developed and tweaked and developed until we got the blend just right. We tested hundreds of recipes, experimenting and fine-tuning until everything tasted just perfect. Nothing thrills me more than to tell you *SomerSweet is here!*

Now you really can have your cake and eat it, too! This is remarkable! SomerSweet is a delicious blend including fructose and sweet fibers. You know,

fiber . . . the stuff your body needs anyway? Well, SomerSweet gives you fiber your body needs with the sweetness your taste buds crave. There's no aftertaste, just a clean sweet taste that is perfect for making guilt-free treats.

Unlike many other products I've tried, Somer-Sweet is great for baking . . . so now you can also *make* your cake and eat it, too! The fibers in the blend provide the bulking ingredient for baking, so SomerSweet bakes just like sugar! Wait until you try my Chocolate Bundt Cake. It's light and airy and made without refined sugar. No more rock-hard cakes made with sugar substitutes . . . SomerSweet will change all of that.

SomerSweet is good for those of us who are on a low-carbohydrate program, or anyone else who understands the health benefits of a low-sugar diet. Best of all, SomerSweet tastes great. Really great! The only way you'll know you're not eating sugar is that you'll feel better, you'll look better, and you won't have that guilty look on your face! Just a big SomerSweet smile.

What impresses me most about SomerSweet is that it is a dream to cook with. In fact, in *Eat, Cheat, and Melt the Fat Away,* I told you that SomerSweet was made from fructose derived from lo han, a fruit grown in China. After the book went to print, I found much better ingredients for SomerSweet that hold up miraculously in the cooking process. SomerSweet cooks like a dream! You can heat it, you can freeze it, you can boil it, bake it, fry it, broil it, and toast it. In this dessert book you'll see how beautifully it works to create delicious cakes, puddings, tarts, ice cream, and more. You can even caramelize it to make a perfect caramelized top for crème brûlée! All of these sinful desserts are now Somersized because of this new product, SomerSweet!

So now that we have numerous Somersize desserts, does that mean we can eat as much as we want and still lose weight? To answer that question, I have divided the desserts into three categories: Level One, Almost Level One, and Level Two. Level One is the weight-loss portion of the program where you eat almost no sugar and you do not combine proteins and fats with carbohydrates. You will find several new Level One desserts that you may eat freely, like Decaf Coffee Granita with Perfectly Whipped Cream—a delightful dessert after a Pro/Fats meal, or as a snack in the afternoon. I have also reprised my New York–Style Cheesecake recipe, which appeared in my first Somersize book, *Eat Great, Lose Weight,* because now we can make it with SomerSweet! Plus, Lemon Zabaglione, Caramel Cheesecake, and more! Yum! And you're still losing weight!

When you are starting out on Level One, stick to the Level One desserts only. These are the only desserts in this book that will not disrupt your progress at all. Technically, because these desserts are made only with Pro/Fats, you may eat until you feel satisfied. Have a lovely portion of a dessert and enjoy every bite. Should you eat the whole cheesecake just because it is Level One? Of course not. We are retraining our metabolism to be healthy and normal. Don't use these delicious SomerSweet desserts to turn yourself into a little piglet (like me). Plus, the desserts are so rich, you will not want more than a small portion. The only reason we overeat desserts is because sugar creates a false craving for more sugar. With SomerSweet you'll feel satisfied with one rich and sinful portion.

The new category I have defined is called Almost Level One. Once you have started losing weight steadily on Level One, you may continue to enjoy Level One desserts, plus you may incorporate a moderate amount of Almost Level One desserts. Please wait to partake in Almost Level One desserts until your weight loss is in full swing. We do not want to halt your progress! Before "The Melt" has begun, you must be very careful not to stray from Level One guidelines. Once your body begins melting your fat as your energy source, you may test your progress with the occasional Almost Level One dessert.

Most of the desserts in the Almost Level One group are made of Pro/Fats with a small amount of a Funky Food, such as unsweetened chocolate or a bit of cornstarch. Chocolate, or cocoa without sugar, is still a Funky Food because it has a small amount of carbohydrate and it has caffeine. As you know from reading my Somersize books, carbohydrates and caffeine can both cause an insulin response. If you are steadily losing weight, your body can probably handle the small amount of imbalance that will occur due to the addition of a small portion of unsweetened chocolate. That is why I allow a moderate amount of Almost Level One desserts when you are still losing weight on Level One. You'll love Dark Chocolate Mousse, Chocolate Cheesecake, Vanilla Custard with Berries, and more!

When you reach your goal weight, you graduate to the maintenance portion of Somersizing, called Level Two. On Level Two you will continue eating Level One and Almost Level One desserts, plus you may incorporate Level Two desserts in moderation. Now you have retrained your metabolism by cleaning out all of the stored sugar in your cells. Your body can handle a moderate amount of imbalance created by Funky Foods and combinations of Pro/Fats with Carbos. How about Wild Mountain Blueberry Pie? Dig in! How about Strawberry Custard Tart with Whole Wheat Pastry Crust? You'll love it! Just remember not to overdo it, or you'll have to go back to Level One until you get your balance back.

The wonderful thing about SomerSweet is that it won't start the craving cycle that sugar does. We're all familiar with sugar highs and lows. When you eat sugar, your blood sugar rises. To balance the blood sugar, your body secretes the hormone insulin (the fat-storing hormone). Insulin balances the blood sugar and decides if the sugar should be burned as fuel or stored as fat. Often your body oversecretes insulin, which lowers your blood sugar even below its starting point. At this point we hit that familiar "sugar low" and once again reach for something sweet or caffeinated to perk us up. This type of sugar bingeing creates a craving cycle that keeps us reaching for sweets all day long. With real sugar, one

cookie or one piece of cake is never enough. One chocolate is never enough.

After you eat a dessert with SomerSweet, you won't be wishing for more an hour later, because reasonable amounts of SomerSweet will not spike your insulin level. Moderating your insulin is the key to losing weight. Food cannot be stored as fat without the presence of insulin. That is why when we Somersize, we can feast, as long as the foods do not trigger a big insulin response. Now, with my new SomerSweet we can also enjoy delicious desserts! It feels so great to eat one SomerSweet Chocolate Truffle in the afternoon and not feel the need to go back for two, three, or four more. I truly feel satisfied after one.

So enjoy your Somersize desserts made with SomerSweet. You and your family and your guests will love them!

TIPS

Here are a few tips that will help you as you prepare the following desserts.

When buying ingredients, purchase the highest quality you can afford, especially when it comes to chocolate. Regular baking chocolate from the grocery store will work, but high-quality chocolate will make your desserts taste that much better. And keep your eyes peeled for the introduction of my new line of SomerSweet Chocolate Bars, including unsweetened chocolate for baking.

Also, use pure vanilla extract, not imitation vanilla. Pure vanilla extract is made from chopped beans mixed with alcohol and water to extract the flavor. Imitation vanilla flavoring is mostly artificial flavorings made with chemicals and often has a harsh quality that leaves a bitter aftertaste.

Better yet, use real vanilla beans when called for. They are expensive but lend unparalleled flavor.

Use real cream and real unsalted butter. The highest-quality ingredients make your food taste best.

Always read the entire recipe before you begin cooking. That way you'll have an idea of what's coming up next and there won't be any surprises, like the need for a specific piece of equipment.

Lay out all the ingredients and equipment for each recipe before you begin—bowls, electric mixers, whisks, measuring spoons, etc. Timing can be critical when you are baking, so you want everything nearby on the counter.

Make sure your ingredients are fresh. Obviously, your eggs and cream should be fresh, but also your baking powder, baking soda, and flour. Many of us have tins of baking powder that have been in the pantry for a decade! When they age, many ingredients lose their efficacy. Treat yourself and restock your baking ingredients.

I have given you substitutions for SomerSweet so that you may make the recipes in this book with saccharin or sugar instead. Once you taste SomerSweet, I'm certain you won't want to use anything else, but I just wanted to give you other options in case you do not have access to SomerSweet. Also, if you'd like to try SomerSweet with your other favorite recipes, simply use it instead of sugar. Be sure to follow the equivalency chart on the SomerSweet label.

Good luck, and happy baking!

SOMERSWEET IS COMING SOON TO STORES AND IS AVAILABLE NOW AT SUZANNESOMERS.COM

LEVEL ONE

DESSERTS

DECAF COFFEE GRANITA with PERFECTLY WHIPPED CREAM

LEVEL ONE / Serves 6–8

This just might be my favorite recipe in the whole book. It's so easy to make and it's so delicious. A perfect Level One dessert. *Granita* is the Italian word for a dessert ice. I've added heavy cream to this classic recipe to make it even smoother. Traditionally, ices are stirred frequently while they freeze to produce a slightly granular texture. Allow three or four hours to complete the granita.

Whisk together the boiling water and decaf coffee in a large mixing bowl. Stir in the cream and SomerSweet.

Cool to room temperature. Place in a 9×9-inch ovenproof Pyrex baking dish and place in the freezer. As soon as ice appears on the edges (about 3 hours), stir the mixture with a fork. Continue to stir and break up ice every hour until mixture is slushy. Use a fork to flake the granita into serving dishes. Top with a dollop of Perfectly Whipped Cream.

PERFECTLY WHIPPED CREAM

LEVEL ONE / Makes about 3 cups

With an electric mixer, whip the cream until it starts to thicken. Add the vanilla and SomerSweet. Continue whipping until soft peaks form.

GRANITA
2 cups boiling water
¼ cup strong brewed decaf coffee
2 cups heavy cream
3 tablespoons SomerSweet
1 recipe Perfectly Whipped Cream (below)

SOMERSWEET SUBSTITUTIONS
saccharin: 1 tablespoon plus 2 teaspoons
sugar: ¾ cup

PERFECTLY WHIPPED CREAM
2 cups whipping cream
1 teaspoon vanilla
2 teaspoons SomerSweet

SOMERSWEET SUBSTITUTIONS
saccharin: 1½ teaspoons
powdered sugar: 2 tablespoons

CRÈME BRÛLÉE

LEVEL ONE / Serves 8

This classic dessert is simply the best-tasting custard, topped with caramelized sugar. To caramelize the SomerSweet, you can use a kitchen torch, available at cooking stores, or you can place the crème brûlée under the broiler until it's brown and crusty. There's nothing like taking your spoon and tapping through the hard caramel crust to the smooth, creamy custard. By the way, in case you forgot, you're still losing weight.

Preheat oven to 350°.

Lightly butter eight 3-ounce ramekins or heatproof custard cups.

Lightly whisk the egg yolks together with 1 tablespoon SomerSweet in a mixing bowl until frothy.

Heat the cream in a small saucepan until just scalded. Whisk the hot cream into the egg mixture.

Add the vanilla extract or the scrapings from the inside of the vanilla bean.

Pour the custard batter into the buttered ramekins. Place the ramekins in a roasting pan. At the oven door, add hot water to the bottom of the pan until the water comes halfway up the sides of the ramekins.

This is a water bath, which helps keep the custard from curdling, cracking, or breaking.

Bake until the custard starts to set up, about 20 minutes. Remove the ramekins from the water bath. Cover with plastic wrap and refrigerate until firm, about 2 hours.

When ready to serve, sprinkle the remaining ¼ cup SomerSweet evenly over the tops of the custards.

To caramelize the tops, use a kitchen propane torch or place the ramekins under a hot broiler, 3 inches from the heat, until the SomerSweet browns.

Unsalted butter for the ramekins or cups
6 large egg yolks
1 tablespoon SomerSweet
2¼ cups cream
2 tablespoons vanilla or 1 vanilla bean, split lengthwise and scraped
¼ cup SomerSweet for topping

SOMERSWEET SUBSTITUTIONS
sugar: 4 tablespoons to mix with egg yolks; 5 tablespoons to sprinkle evenly over the tops of the custards
This recipe cannot be made with saccharin.

ORANGE SOUFFLÉ

LEVEL ONE / Serves 4

This baked soufflé is perfection. It is light and airy. New cooks often think soufflés are difficult, but, in fact, you'll find this recipe easy and delicious. This soufflé makes a tasty and impressive Level One dessert.

Preheat oven to 450°.

Butter a 1-quart soufflé dish.

Beat the egg yolks and 1 tablespoon of SomerSweet (or 2 teaspoons saccharin, or ¼ cup sugar) until light and tripled in volume, about 6–8 minutes. Add the orange extract, orange zest, and heavy cream. Continue to beat for another minute.

In another bowl, beat egg whites until frothy. Add 2 teaspoons Somer-Sweet (or 1 teaspoon saccharin or ¼ cup sugar) and beat until stiff peaks form.

Gently fold the egg whites into the yolk mixture until well incorporated. Transfer to the soufflé dish and bake for 15–20 minutes. Serve immediately.

NOTE: For a straighter, taller soufflé, add a parchment paper collar before baking: Cut a 24-inch-long piece of parchment paper. Fold it in half. It will be about 8 inches wide. Butter it on one side. Wrap it around the outside of the soufflé dish, with the buttered side against the dish. Secure it with a piece of string or staple it together. Bake as usual and remove immediately before serving.

Unsalted butter for the soufflé dish
6 large egg yolks at room temperature
1 tablespoon SomerSweet
2 teaspoons orange extract
2 teaspoons orange zest
¼ cup heavy cream
6 large egg whites at room temperature
2 teaspoons SomerSweet

SOMERSWEET SUBSTITUTIONS
saccharin: 1 tablespoon
sugar: ½ cup

RASPBERRY SORBET

LEVEL ONE / Makes about 2 cups

Most store-bought sorbets are made with a ton of sugar or sweeteners. Not mine. This is pure fruit and SomerSweet. A perfect midafternoon treat. You'll need an ice cream maker for this recipe.

Place all the ingredients in a food processor or blender and blend until smooth. Taste and add more SomerSweet if needed.

Place in an ice cream maker and freeze according to the manufacturer's directions.

2⅔ cups fresh or frozen raspberries
⅓ cup water
2 tablespoons or more SomerSweet, depending on the sweetness of your berries
2 tablespoons lemon juice

SOMERSWEET SUBSTITUTIONS
saccharin: 1 tablespoon plus 1 teaspoon, or more
sugar: ½ cup, or more, depending on the sweetness of your berries

PEACH SORBET

LEVEL ONE / Makes about 3 cups

I've always loved peaches. Alan and I have a peach tree in Palm Springs, and when we get a big harvest, I make peach everything—including this divine Peach Sorbet. We sit by the pool and feed one another. When peaches are out of season, the frozen ones work great. You'll need an ice cream maker for this recipe.

Place all the ingredients in a food processor or blender and blend until smooth. Taste and add more SomerSweet if needed.

Place in an ice cream maker and freeze according to the manufacturer's directions.

2¼ cups sliced peaches,
    fresh or frozen and
    thawed
⅓ cup water
2 tablespoons plus
    2 teaspoons SomerSweet
2 tablespoons lemon juice

SOMERSWEET SUBSTITUTIONS
saccharin: 1 tablespoon plus 2
   teaspoons
sugar: ¾ cup

NEW YORK–STYLE CHEESECAKE

LEVEL ONE / Serves 8–10

It's hard to believe, but my classic, creamy, crustless cheesecake is a Level One dessert—perfect for everyday Somersizing or to serve to your finest company. If you'd like to serve it with Raspberry Coulis, it becomes an Almost Level One dessert.

Preheat oven to 350°.

Butter the sides and bottom of a 9-inch springform pan. Line the bottom with a double thickness of waxed paper. Lay two 24-inch-long pieces of aluminum foil on a work surface to make an **X**.

Place the springform pan in the center of the foil and fold up around the sides to form a waterproof jacket.

In a large mixing bowl beat the cream cheese and SomerSweet until light and fluffy. Add the eggs one at a time, beating well after each addition. Add sour cream, lemon juice, lemon zest, and vanilla. Mix until smooth.

Pour the batter into the prepared pan and place in a large roasting pan. At the door of the oven, pour enough hot water into the roasting pan to surround the cheesecake with one inch of water. This is a water bath, which helps keep the cheesecake from cracking and curdling.

Bake for 1 hour. Turn off the oven and let cool, for an additional hour, without opening the door. Remove the cheesecake from the water bath and cool to room temperature. Cover with plastic wrap. Refrigerate in the springform pan overnight.

Run a warm knife around the edges of the cheesecake before you release the springform. Transfer cheesecake to a serving dish.

RASPBERRY COULIS

LEVEL ONE / Makes 1 cup

Coulis is a French version of a fruit puree. This simple dessert sauce is strained to eliminate the seeds. It is delightful over ice cream, or to pool under cheesecake or chocolate cake.

Place all the ingredients in a food processor and pulse until pureed. Push the puree through a fine-mesh sieve to remove seeds. If you want the coulis thinner, adjust the consistency with 1–2 tablespoons water.

To serve warm, heat the strained puree in a saucepan, whisking in 1–2 tablespoons of unsalted butter for a glossy sheen.

CHEESECAKE

Unsalted butter for the pan

3 (8-ounce) packages cream cheese at room temperature

2 tablespoons SomerSweet

3 large eggs at room temperature

1 cup sour cream

1½ tablespoons freshly squeezed lemon juice

1 teaspoon lemon zest

1 teaspoon vanilla

SOMERSWEET SUBSTITUTIONS
saccharin: 1 tablespoon
sugar: ¾ cup

RASPBERRY COULIS

2 (6-ounce) baskets of raspberries, fresh, or 12 ounces frozen, completely thawed

2–3 teaspoons SomerSweet

1 tablespoon lemon juice

1–2 tablespoons unsalted butter (optional)

SOMERSWEET SUBSTITUTIONS
saccharin: 2 teaspoons
sugar: ¼ cup or more, depending on the sweetness of the berries

CARAMEL CHEESECAKE

LEVEL ONE / Serves 8–10

It's beautiful. It's rich. It's creamy. It's Level One. It's a dream.

Preheat oven to 350°.

Butter the sides and bottom of a 9-inch springform pan. Line the bottom with a double thickness of waxed paper. Lay two 24-inch-long pieces of aluminum foil on a work surface to make an X.

Place the springform pan in the center of the foil and fold up around the sides to form a waterproof jacket.

Prepare the New York–Style Cheesecake filling as directed, omitting the lemon juice and lemon zest.

Prepare 1½ cups Caramel Sauce (1½ times the recipe).

Pour half of the cheesecake batter into the prepared pan. Drizzle all over with half of the caramel sauce. Add the remaining cheesecake batter. Drizzle the remainder of the caramel sauce on top of the batter. Using a toothpick or bamboo skewer, swirl the sauce into the cheesecake to create a marbled effect.

Bake as for New York–Style Cheesecake.

CARAMEL SAUCE

Level One / Makes about 1 cup

The most amazing thing about SomerSweet is that it caramelizes like real sugar! Wait until you try this gooey Caramel Sauce on cheesecake or ice cream. It's divine.

Heat the SomerSweet and water in a heavy-bottomed saucepan over low heat until dissolved. Bring to a boil and continue to cook for 4½ minutes or until the liquid turns golden brown and frothy.

Remove from the heat and slowly pour in the cream, stirring constantly. Whisk in the butter until smooth. Cool to room temperature, then refrigerate.

CHEESECAKE
1 recipe New York-Style Cheesecake (page 25), omitting lemon juice and lemon zest
1½ cups Caramel Sauce (below)

CARAMEL SAUCE
¼ cup plus 2 tablespoons SomerSweet
¼ cup plus 2 tablespoons water
¾ cup heavy cream
4 tablespoons (½ stick) unsalted butter at room temperature

SOMERSWEET SUBSTITUTION
sugar: ¼ cup plus 2 tablespoons
This recipe cannot be made with saccharin.

CAPPUCCINO CHEESECAKE
LEVEL ONE / Serves 8–10

There's nothing like a spoonful of SomerSweet stirred into a frothy cappuccino. The combined flavors are divine. Now you can have that same fantastic taste in this creamy Cappuccino Cheesecake.

Preheat oven to 350°.

Butter the sides and bottom of a 9-inch springform pan. Line the bottom with a double thickness of waxed paper. Lay two 24-inch-long pieces of aluminum foil on a work surface to make an X. Place the pan in the center of the foil and fold up around the sides to form a waterproof jacket.

In a large mixing bowl beat the cream cheese and SomerSweet until light and fluffy. Add the eggs one at a time, beating well after each addition. Add the sour cream and vanilla. Mix until smooth.

Dissolve the instant coffee in ½ cup of hot water. Add to the cream cheese mixture and mix well.

Pour the batter into the prepared pan and place in a large roasting pan. At the door of the oven, pour enough hot water into the roasting pan to surround the cheesecake pan with one inch of water. This is a water bath, which helps prevent the cheesecake from curdling, breaking, or cracking.

Bake for 1 hour. Turn off the oven and let the cheesecake cool for an additional hour without opening the door.

Cover the baked cheesecake with plastic wrap. Refrigerate overnight. To unmold, run a warm knife around the edge of the cheesecake and transfer the cheesecake to a serving dish. Garnish with Perfectly Whipped Cream and decaf coffee beans.

Unsalted butter for the pan
3 (8-ounce) packages cream cheese at room temperature
¼ cup SomerSweet
3 large eggs at room temperature
¾ cup sour cream
1 tablespoon vanilla
6 tablespoons instant decaf coffee
½ cup hot water
Perfectly Whipped Cream (page 15)
8–10 decaf coffee beans

SOMERSWEET SUBSTITUTIONS
saccharin: 2 tablespoons plus 1 teaspoon
sugar: 1 cup

29

LEMON ZABAGLIONE

LEVEL ONE / Serves 6

One of Italy's greatest gifts to the world is zabaglione, a classic dessert made with Marsala wine. My recipe is a twist on the traditional. Instead of using Marsala, I use fresh lemon juice. The taste is magical. Traditionally it is served warm in dessert cups, garnished with a piece of fresh mint, or over fresh berries. If you serve this over berries it becomes an Almost Level One dessert.

Heat one inch of water to a simmer in a 3-quart saucepan (or the bottom of a double boiler). Place the eggs, egg yolks, and SomerSweet in a medium-sized stainless steel bowl (or the top of a double boiler) and add the lemon juice.

Place the bowl over the simmering water, not letting the bottom of the bowl touch the water. Whisk vigorously to combine, until the eggs are light and foamy and have thickened, about 8–9 minutes.

Serve immediately, in small dishes or glasses.

Variation:
COLD CREAMY LEMON ZABAGLIONE

Instead of serving the sauce warm, let it cool to room temperature and add ¾ cup heavy cream that has been whipped to soft peaks. Chill and serve.

4 large eggs
4 large egg yolks
3 tablespoons SomerSweet
½ cup fresh squeezed
   lemon juice (about
   4 lemons)

SOMERSWEET SUBSTITUTIONS
saccharin: 1 tablespoon plus
   2 teaspoons
sugar: ¾ cup

almost
LEVEL ONE

DESSERTS

STEAMED CHOCOLATE PUDDING

ALMOST LEVEL ONE / Serves 8–10

My brother-in-law, Lewis, introduced me to steamed puddings several Christmases ago. He is from Australia, and puddings are a way of life "down under." I use an antique pudding mold. It's a classic French *bombe* or arched shape. But a bowl works great, too.

To prepare the mold:

Use 1 tablespoon of the butter to grease a 1-quart pudding mold (or bowl, see note below), including the inside of the lid.

Sprinkle 1 tablespoon of the Somer-Sweet into the mold, hold the lid on tight, and shake.

To make the pudding:

Slice the vanilla bean lengthwise with a paring knife and scrape the insides into a small heavy saucepan. Place the pod in as well. (Or add the vanilla extract.) Add the cream and the chocolate. Warm over low heat, stirring occasionally, until the chocolate is melted. Set aside.

Melt the remaining 3 tablespoons butter in another saucepan and add the flour. Cook over low heat about 1 minute, until blended. Stirring continuously, slowly add the cream and chocolate mixture. Remove the vanilla bean pod.

Place the egg yolks and the remaining SomerSweet in a large mixing bowl. Beat until thick and lemon colored. Slowly whisk in the warm chocolate mixture. Add the brandy and mix well.

Pour the egg whites into a clean bowl and beat with an electric mixer until stiff. Beat ¾ cup of the egg whites into the chocolate mixture. Then gently fold in the remaining egg whites.

Carefully pour the pudding into the mold and place the lid on securely. Place the mold on a rack in a large stockpot filled with enough water to come halfway up the sides of the mold. Cover and simmer on low heat for 1 hour and 15 minutes.

Remove the pudding mold from the pot and cool for 10 minutes. To unmold, remove the lid and gently shake until the pudding pulls away from the sides. Carefully invert onto a serving plate. (If it sticks, gently tap the mold with a wooden spoon.)

Serve with Perfectly Whipped Cream.

NOTE: If you don't have a mold, use a stainless steel kitchen bowl 8 inches in diameter and about 3 inches deep. For a lid, cut four 12-inch foil squares and layer them over the top. Take a string and tie it around the foil to secure the flaps so no water gets in. Cook as directed.

4 tablespoons unsalted butter, separated
¼ cup plus 3 tablespoons SomerSweet
1 vanilla bean or 1 teaspoon vanilla
1½ cups heavy cream
6 ounces (6 squares) unsweetened baking chocolate
2 tablespoons all-purpose whole wheat flour
5 large eggs, separated
2 tablespoons brandy
Perfectly Whipped Cream (page 15)

SOMERSWEET SUBSTITUTIONS
saccharin: ¼ cup
sugar: use 6 ounces of sweetened baking chocolate

VANILLA CUSTARD WITH BERRIES

ALMOST LEVEL ONE / Serves 4

This delicious custard makes a wonderful dessert by itself or with fresh berries. Serve the vanilla custard warm or cold, depending on the time of year.

Combine the SomerSweet, cream, and cornstarch in a heavy-bottomed saucepan. Heat on medium high, stirring constantly, until boiling. Continue to cook for about 1 minute. Turn the heat down to low and continue stirring for another minute. Set aside to cool.

Lightly whisk the egg yolks in a stainless steel bowl. Pour the hot cream mixture over the yolks. Whisk.

Return the eggs and cream to the pan and stir over medium heat until thick and smooth, about 2 minutes.

Remove from the heat and add the vanilla. Serve immediately or chill.

Fill champagne or parfait glasses with fresh berries and layer the custard on top. Garnish with a few more berries.

1 tablespoon plus
   1 teaspoon SomerSweet
2½ cups heavy cream
¼ cup cornstarch
4 large egg yolks
½ teaspoon vanilla
2 baskets of fresh berries

SOMERSWEET SUBSTITUTIONS
saccharin: 2 teaspoons
sugar: ⅓ cup

CHOCOLATE LAYER CAKE
ALMOST LEVEL ONE / Serves 8–10

This cake tastes like it's made with flour, but it's not! Just a pinch of baking soda. If you want, you can double the recipe to make a four-layer cake, perfect for special occasions. Be sure to divide the batter evenly between two 9-inch pans.

Preheat oven to 400°.

Cover the bottom of a 9-inch spring-form pan with two squares of waxed paper.

Grease the waxed paper and sides with butter. Snap the springform sides into place and trim the excess paper. Set aside.

In a heavy-bottomed saucepan, melt the chocolate and butter over low heat, stirring until smooth. Set aside to cool slightly.

Place the eggs in a large bowl and beat at high speed until tripled in volume, about 8 minutes. Add the Somer-Sweet, vanilla, and baking soda. Beat for 30 seconds.

Mix ⅓ of the egg mixture into the chocolate-butter mixture. Then fold the chocolate butter into the remaining egg mixture until combined. Spoon the batter into the pan and bake for 15 minutes.

Remove the pan from the oven and allow the cake to cool completely. Release the springform and carefully peel off the wax paper.

To layer the cake:

Using a serrated knife, cut the cake horizontally into two layers. Dollop the buttercream onto the center of the bottom layer, using a flat frosting spatula, and spread evenly to within ½ inch of the cake's edge. Place the second layer on top and refrigerate 20 minutes.

To frost the cake:

Transfer the cake to a cooling rack set over a cookie sheet.

Heat the ganache in a microwavable glass measuring cup or on the stovetop in a heavy-bottomed saucepan over low heat until it is melted to the consistency of cream. Slowly pour the ganache over the top and sides of the cake, tilting the cooling rack to control the direction of the flow. Refrigerate until firm.

Unsalted butter for the cake pan
6 ounces (6 squares) unsweetened chocolate
1 stick plus 2 tablespoons unsalted butter
6 large eggs at room temperature
½ cup SomerSweet
1 tablespoon vanilla
¼ teaspoon baking soda
1 recipe Chocolate Buttercream (page 41)
1 recipe Chocolate Ganache (page 41)

SOMERSWEET SUBSTITUTIONS
saccharin: ¼ cup
sugar: use 6 ounces of sweetened chocolate

CHOCOLATE BUTTERCREAM

Almost Level One / Fills one layer cake

This recipe is enough to fill one Chocolate Layer Cake, or for you to sit down with a spoon and be a little pig.

Heat the cream in a heavy-bottomed saucepan until hot but not boiling. Place the chocolate in a bowl and pour the hot cream over it. Stir until the chocolate is completely melted and smooth. Add the SomerSweet, vanilla, and baking soda. Stir thoroughly.

Place in the refrigerator and cool to the consistency of soft butter. Place the softened butter in a mixing bowl and beat until light and fluffy. Add the cooled chocolate mixture and continue to beat until creamy. Refrigerate until ready to use.

CHOCOLATE GANACHE

Almost Level One / Makes enough to frost one Chocolate Layer Cake

The easiest and most delicious way to frost a cake is to pour the melted chocolate mixture over the cake and then let it set to a smooth, glossy finish. When frosting your cake, if any ganache has dripped onto the cookie sheet, save it. The ganache can be refrigerated, reheated, and used again.

Place the chocolate in a blender or the bowl of a food processor and set aside.

Heat the cream in a heavy-bottomed saucepan until hot but not boiling.

Pour the hot cream over the chocolate and pulse or process until smooth. Add the SomerSweet, vanilla, and baking soda. Cool slightly until the ganache is the consistency of heavy cream. Slowly pour the ganache over the top and sides of the cake, smoothing with a spatula. Refrigerate until firm. If you are not going to use the ganache right away, you must refrigerate it until needed. Then reheat in a double boiler until it is the consistency of heavy cream. Or heat in a microwave for about 30 seconds.

CHOCOLATE BUTTERCREAM
¾ cup heavy cream
1½ ounces (1½ squares) unsweetened chocolate, chopped into ¼-inch pieces
2 teaspoons SomerSweet
1 teaspoon vanilla
Pinch baking soda
2 sticks unsalted butter, softened

SOMERSWEET SUBSTITUTIONS
saccharin: 1½ teaspoons
sugar: 1 tablespoon

CHOCOLATE GANACHE
3 ounces (3 squares) unsweetened chocolate, chopped into ¼-inch pieces
1¼ cups heavy cream
2 teaspoons SomerSweet
1 teaspoon vanilla
Pinch baking soda

SOMERSWEET SUBSTITUTIONS
saccharin: 1 teaspoon
sugar: ¼ cup

CARAMEL PUDDING PARFAIT

ALMOST LEVEL ONE / Serves 4

My son Bruce has always loved pudding. I used to make butterscotch pudding for him, but it was loaded with sugar. Now I can make his delicious childhood favorite with no sugar at all!

In a medium saucepan, combine the cornstarch and ⅓ of the cream with a wooden spoon. Gradually stir in the rest of the cream, stirring constantly.

Cook over medium heat, stirring consistently until the mixture boils and thickens.

In a mixing bowl lightly beat the egg yolks with the SomerSweet. Add about ⅓ of the hot cream mixture to the egg yolks and blend.

Return the egg mixture to the rest of the thickened cream and stir well.

Remove from heat. And the vanilla, 1 recipe Caramel Sauce, and the butter. Stir until combined.

To assemble, spoon the remaining Caramel Sauce into the bottom of 4 individual cups or glasses. Add the pudding. Cool slightly and top with Perfectly Whipped Cream before serving.

Store in the refrigerator.

CARAMEL SAUCE

Level One / Makes about ¾ cup

When I first found SomerSweet, I was thrilled to find out that it caramelizes. This versatile sauce can be served on cheesecake, chocolate cake, ice cream, and used to make Caramel Pudding Parfait.

Dissolve the SomerSweet in the water in a small heavy-bottomed saucepan. Bring to a boil and continue to cook, without stirring, for 5–8 minutes, until the liquid turns golden brown and frothy. Take care not to let the mixture burn.

Remove from heat and slowly pour in the cream, whisking constantly. Return to low heat and whisk gently until sauce is smooth. Whisk in the butter. Remove from heat. Sauce will thicken as it cools. Cool to room temperature and refrigerate.

PUDDING

2 tablespoons cornstarch
2 cups heavy cream
4 large egg yolks
1 tablespoon SomerSweet
2 teaspoons vanilla
2 recipes Caramel Sauce
1 tablespoon unsalted butter
Perfectly Whipped Cream
    (page 15)

SOMERSWEET SUBSTITUTIONS
saccharin: 2½ teaspoons
sugar: ⅓ cup

CARAMEL SAUCE

¼ cup SomerSweet
¼ cup plus 2 tablespoons
    water
½ cup heavy cream
4 tablespoons (½ stick)
    unsalted butter at room
    temperature

SOMERSWEET SUBSTITUTION
sugar: ¼ cup plus
    2 tablespoons
This recipe cannot be made
    with saccharin.

SOMERSWEET TRUFFLES—Chocolate, Orange, and Cappuccino

ALMOST LEVEL ONE / Makes about 30 1-ounce truffles

This recipe for my SomerSweet Truffles has started a craze! If you don't want to make them, you can purchase a box on my Web site at SuzanneSomers.com. Either way, you won't believe you can bite into these gooey, rich chocolate truffles without the accompanying guilt! Go ahead; they're made with SomerSweet, so you really can eat them and still control your weight. Use the best-quality unsweetened chocolate you can afford. After just one bite, you'll be dancing in the streets.

CHOCOLATE TRUFFLES

Place the chopped chocolate in the bowl of a food processor or blender. Heat the cream in a saucepan over medium heat until small bubbles appear around the edge.

Pour the cream over the chocolate and allow to stand for 30 seconds. Blend until the mixture is smooth.

Add the vanilla, SomerSweet, and a pinch of baking soda.

Transfer the mixture to a shallow dish and refrigerate until firm, at least 1 hour.

Using a 1-ounce scoop or a tablespoon, scoop balls of chocolate and place on a baking sheet. Refrigerate for about 30 minutes.

When chilled, roll each truffle in the palm of your hand into a perfect round ball.

Drop the truffles into the sweetened cocoa powder to coat the exterior.

Store the truffles in the refrigerator in an airtight container.

Variations:

ORANGE TRUFFLES

Omit vanilla and add ½ teaspoon orange extract.

CAPPUCCINO TRUFFLES

Pour the coffee into the food processor or blender with the chopped chocolate. Continue with the main recipe for truffles, beginning with "Heat the cream in a saucepan . . ."

CHOCOLATE TRUFFLES
6 ounces (6 squares) unsweetened chocolate, chopped into small pieces
1½ cups heavy cream
¾ teaspoon vanilla
2 tablespoons plus ½ teaspoon SomerSweet
Pinch baking soda
¼ cup unsweetened cocoa powder mixed with 2 tablespoons SomerSweet for dusting finished truffles

SOMERSWEET SUBSTITUTIONS
saccharin: 2 teaspoons for truffles plus 1 tablespoon for dusting
sugar: use 18 ounces semi-sweet chocolate chips for truffles plus ¼ cup sugar to sweeten the cocoa

ORANGE TRUFFLES
½ teaspoon orange extract

CAPPUCCINO TRUFFLES
¼ cup prepared instant decaf coffee or ¼ cup brewed decaf coffee

HOT FUDGE SUNDAE

ALMOST LEVEL ONE / Makes about 4 sundaes

I've had a passionate affair with ice cream for more than fifty years. Now, with my new SomerSweet, it's the treat I eat to lose weight. Oh my, I love this stuff! My ice cream is made with cream instead of milk, so it's very rich. And my Hot Fudge will make you grin like a kid. It's a good time to invest in an ice cream maker.

Pour the cream and water into a saucepan. Heat until hot but not boiling. Remove from heat.

Place the egg yolks in a mixing bowl. Pour the hot cream mixture over the eggs, whisking constantly.

Return to low heat and stir consistently with a wooden spoon until the mixture thickens and coats the back of the spoon. Do not let the mixture boil.

Split the vanilla beans lengthwise and scrape the insides. Add the vanilla bean scrapings (or the vanilla extract) and SomerSweet to the hot mixture and stir.

Transfer the mixture to a bowl, cover the surface of the custard with waxed paper, and cool to room temperature. Chill for 2 hours.

Pour the chilled custard into a chilled ice cream maker and follow the manufacturer's directions.

HOT FUDGE SAUCE

Whisk the SomerSweet and water in a small heavy-bottomed saucepan until dissolved.

Bring to a boil and cook, stirring, for about 4 minutes or until the mixture turns frothy and golden brown. Be careful not to let the mixture burn.

Remove from heat and whisk in the cream. Add the chocolate.

Return to low heat and whisk gently until the mixture is completely smooth. Whisk in the softened butter. Allow to cool slightly before using.

For the sundae:

Place two scoops of Vanilla Bean Ice Cream in a dish. Top with Hot Fudge Sauce. Garnish with Perfectly Whipped Cream.

You can also add Caramel Sauce or Raspberry Coulis.

VANILLA BEAN ICE CREAM
2½ cups heavy cream
½ cup water
8 large egg yolks
2 whole vanilla beans, or
 1 tablespoon vanilla
3 tablespoons SomerSweet

SOMERSWEET SUBSTITUTIONS
saccharin: 1 tablespoon
sugar: ¾ cup

HOT FUDGE SAUCE
¼ cup plus 2 tablespoons
 SomerSweet
¼ cup plus 2 tablespoons
 water
¾ cup plus 3 tablespoons
 heavy cream
2 ounces (2 squares)
 unsweetened chocolate,
 chopped into ½-inch
 pieces
4 tablespoons (½ stick)
 butter, softened

GARNISH
Perfectly Whipped Cream
 (page 15)
Caramel Sauce (page 27)
Raspberry Coulis (page 25)

SOMERSWEET SUBSTITUTION
This recipe cannot be made
 with saccharin.

CARAMEL SWIRL CHOCOLATE CHUNK ICE CREAM

ALMOST LEVEL ONE / Makes about 1 pint

I've had such fun coming up with ice cream recipes for all of us to enjoy. This one starts with my fabulous Vanilla Bean Ice Cream and adds a caramel ripple and chocolate chunks. The caramel ripple and the chocolate chunks are sweetened with SomerSweet. Scoop up a bowl and dig in!

To make the chocolate chunks, melt the chocolate, cream, and SomerSweet in a saucepan until smooth. Allow to cool for 5 minutes.

Pour the chocolate mixture onto the back of a clean cookie sheet, smoothing to about ¼ inch thick. Place the cookie sheet in the refrigerator for 30 minutes.

Remove the cookie sheet from the refrigerator and score the chocolate by making crisscross patterns with a knife so that you have ½-inch squares. Leave the chocolate pieces intact on the cookie sheet. Chill or freeze the sheet pan for another 30 minutes or until very firm.

Using a metal spatula, lift the chocolate chunks off the cookie sheet.

Prepare the Vanilla Bean Ice Cream base as directed. Place in an ice cream maker and follow the manufacturer's directions.

For the caramel swirl, drizzle Caramel Sauce into the ice cream during the last 10 minutes of freezing.

Add the chocolate chunks during the last 5 minutes of freezing.

---

1 ounce (1 square) unsweetened chocolate
2 tablespoons heavy cream
1 tablespoon SomerSweet
1 recipe Vanilla Bean Ice Cream (page 47)
1 cup Caramel Sauce (page 27)

SOMERSWEET SUBSTITUTIONS
saccharin for the chocolate chunks: 2 teaspoons
sugar: use semisweet chocolate chips

DARK CHOCOLATE MOUSSE
ALMOST LEVEL ONE / Serves 4

This recipe is so easy. I like to keep some in the refrigerator and have a few spoonfuls whenever I get a craving. Yum!

In a double boiler or microwave, melt the chocolate and butter. To melt chocolate in a microwave, put chocolate and butter in a microwavable bowl and heat for about 30 seconds at low power. Stir and heat until smooth.

With an electric mixer or wire whisk, whip the cream until it starts to become fluffy. Add the cocoa, SomerSweet, brandy, and vanilla to the cream. Continue to whip until the cream forms soft peaks.

Gently fold the cream into the melted chocolate.

Serve immediately or chill.

3 ounces (3 squares) of unsweetened baking chocolate
2 tablespoons unsalted butter
2 cups heavy cream, well chilled
2 tablespoons unsweetened cocoa powder
2 tablespoons SomerSweet
1 tablespoon plus 1 teaspoon brandy (optional)
1 teaspoon vanilla

SOMERSWEET SUBSTITUTIONS
saccharin: 1 tablespoon
sugar: ½ cup

LEMON-SCENTED RICOTTA

ALMOST LEVEL ONE / Serves 6–8

Whole-milk ricotta is technically a Funky Food because it has a small amount of carbohydrates. That is why this is an Almost Level One dessert. Use the best brand of whole-milk ricotta you can buy. I purchased an imported brand from an Italian deli. It makes a world of difference in taste and consistency. This is also great with fresh berries.

Place the cream in a mixing bowl and beat with an electric mixer until soft peaks form.

In another bowl combine the ricotta, SomerSweet, lemon zest, and lemon juice, and beat until fluffy, about five minutes.

Fold the whipped cream into the ricotta mixture until well incorporated.

Spoon into custard cups and refrigerate overnight.

Garnish with lemon zest before serving.

1 cup heavy cream
2 cups whole-milk ricotta
1 tablespoon plus 1
   teaspoon SomerSweet
2 tablespoons finely grated
   lemon zest (reserve half
   for garnish)
1 tablespoon lemon juice

SOMERSWEET SUBSTITUTIONS
saccharin: 3 teaspoons
sugar: 1/3 cup

CHOCOLATE CHEESECAKE

ALMOST LEVEL ONE / Serves 8–10

One more version of my fabulous cheesecake, this time made with chocolate!

Preheat oven to 350°.

Butter a 9-inch springform pan and line the bottom with a double thickness of waxed paper. Lay two 24-inch-long pieces of aluminum foil on a work surface to make an X. Place the pan in the center of the foil and fold up around the sides to form a waterproof jacket.

In a large mixing bowl beat the cream cheese and SomerSweet until light and fluffy. Add the eggs one at a time, beating well after each addition. Add the sour cream and vanilla. Mix well.

Place the chocolate in a stainless steel bowl. In a heavy-bottomed saucepan heat the cream until hot but not boiling. Pour the hot cream over the chocolate and stir until the mixture is smooth. Stir the chocolate mixture into the cheesecake mixture and pour into the prepared pan.

Drizzle Hot Fudge Sauce over the batter and swirl with a toothpick or wooden skewer to make a marbled effect.

Place the springform pan in a large roasting pan. At the door of the oven, pour enough hot water into the roasting pan to surround the pan with one inch of water. This is a water bath, which helps prevent the cheesecake from curdling, breaking, or cracking.

Bake for 1 hour. Turn off the oven and let the cheesecake cool in the oven for an additional hour without opening the door.

Cover the baked cheesecake in the springform pan with plastic wrap and refrigerate overnight. To unmold, run a warm knife around the edge of the cheesecake and transfer the cheesecake to a serving dish.

Variation:
MINI CHEESECAKES

Divide the cheesecake batter between four individual cheesecake molds. Four-inch springform pans can be found in most gourmet cooking stores.

Unsalted butter for the pan
3 (8-ounce) packages cream cheese at room temperature
¼ cup SomerSweet
4 large eggs at room temperature
1 cup sour cream
2 teaspoons vanilla
3 ounces (3 squares) unsweetened chocolate, chopped into ¼-inch pieces
¼ cup heavy cream
½ cup Hot Fudge Sauce (page 47)

SOMERSWEET SUBSTITUTIONS
saccharin for the cheesecake: 2 tablespoons plus 1 teaspoon
sugar for the cheesecake: 1 cup

WILD-BERRY FOOL

ALMOST LEVEL ONE / Serves 4

This delicious dessert takes less time to make than it does to shop for the ingredients. It's a beautiful color and elegant when served in parfait dishes or wineglasses. I purposely use frozen berries so I can make it year-round.

Place the cream and the SomerSweet in a mixing bowl and whip with an electric mixer until soft peaks form. Do not overbeat.

Place the berries in a food processor and pulse until the berries are chunky.

Fold the berries into the whipped cream until well combined. Taste and add more SomerSweet if necessary.

Spoon into serving dishes and chill. Garnish with whole berries before serving.

1 cup heavy cream
1 tablespoon SomerSweet
1 pound mixed frozen
   berries, thawed and
   drained
Berries for garnish

SOMERSWEET SUBSTITUTIONS
saccharin: 2 teaspoons
sugar: ¼ cup

CHOCOLATE KISSES

ALMOST LEVEL ONE / Makes about 30 candies

These delicate little kisses make wonderful party favors.

Place the chocolate in the bowl of a food processor or blender.

Heat the cream in a small heavy-bottomed saucepan until bubbles form around the edge. Pour the hot cream over the chocolate and let set for 2 minutes. Blend until smooth.

Add the peppermint extract and SomerSweet and mix well.

Pour into a stainless steel bowl and refrigerate for 45 minutes to 1 hour, until the mixture is the consistency of soft butter. Place the mixture in a pastry bag fitted with a star tip (no. 7 is a good size). Pipe out kisses onto a cookie sheet lined with parchment paper. Chill for at least 2 hours before serving.

4 ounces (4 squares) unsweetened chocolate, chopped into small chunks
1¼ cups heavy cream
¼ teaspoon peppermint extract
1 tablespoon plus 1 teaspoon SomerSweet

SOMERSWEET SUBSTITUTIONS
saccharin: 1½ teaspoons
sugar: ¼ cup

CHOCOLATE ROULADE

ALMOST LEVEL ONE / Serves 8–12

This is an easy, elegant dessert that will please adults and kids alike. A jelly roll pan is a cookie sheet with sides. I used a 15 × 10-inch nonstick pan that I found at the grocery store.

Preheat oven to 400°.

Butter the sides and bottom of a jelly roll pan (cookie sheet with sides). Line the pan with an 18-inch piece of parchment or waxed paper, allowing the excess to hang over the sides. Butter the paper.

Over low heat, melt the chocolate and butter together in a small heavy-bottomed saucepan, stirring until melted and smooth. Transfer to a mixing bowl and set aside to cool.

In another mixing bowl beat the eggs on high speed until they have tripled in volume, about 8 minutes. Add the SomerSweet, vanilla, and baking soda. Beat for one more minute, until well combined.

Using a spatula, mix ⅓ of the egg mixture into the chocolate mixture. Fold the remaining egg mixture into the chocolate until combined.

Spoon the batter into the prepared pan. Using a spatula, spread the batter evenly. Bake 8–10 minutes, until firm.

Remove from the oven and allow to cool 10 minutes. Sift or sprinkle the top of the cake with 1 tablespoon of the sweetened cocoa. Run a knife or metal spatula around the edge to loosen the cake.

Tear off a sheet of plastic wrap longer than the pan and lay it over the cake. Place a clean dish towel on top of the plastic. The dish towel will help with the rolling process. Put a cutting board on top of the towel and invert the whole cake so that the pan is bottom side up. Remove the pan and carefully peel away the parchment paper.

Fold in any excess plastic wrap and dish towel toward the center of the cake. Roll up the cake jelly roll fashion with the plastic and towel inside. Set aside to cool completely. The cake may crack in places, but it will hold its shape when filled.

To make the filling:

Beat the cream, SomerSweet, and almond extract until stiff.

Carefully unroll the cooled cake and remove the plastic and towel. Spread the cream filling evenly with a spatula. Reroll the cake and set seam side down on a platter. Sprinkle the remaining sweetened cocoa over the roulade.

Slice on the diagonal and serve.

FOR THE CAKE
Unsalted butter for the pan
3 ounces (3 squares) unsweetened chocolate
5 tablespoons unsalted butter
3 large eggs at room temperature
¼ cup SomerSweet
1½ teaspoons vanilla
⅛ teaspoon baking soda
2 tablespoons unsweetened cocoa powder mixed with 1 tablespoon SomerSweet

FOR THE FILLING
1 cup heavy cream
1 teaspoon SomerSweet, or more
1 teaspoon almond extract

SOMERSWEET SUBSTITUTIONS
saccharin for the cake:
   1½ tablespoons
sugar for the cake: 6 ounces
   fine dark chocolate
saccharin for the filling:
   ¾ teaspoon
powdered sugar for the filling:
   1 tablespoon, or more

MOCHA CREAM

This is a satisfying yummy cloud of a dessert. The combination of coffee and chocolate is delicious. I put a big spoonful of mocha cream on a cup of decaf when I want something sweet. I found decaf espresso powder in a local gourmet shop. It's perfect for Somersizing. Or you can use brewed decaf espresso.

Place all the ingredients in a well-chilled bowl. With an electric mixer, beat ingredients together on low speed for 1–2 minutes. Increase the speed to high and whip the cream until thick and billowy.

Serve in chilled dessert glasses. Or place a large dollop on a steaming cup of decaf espresso or French roast.

2 cups heavy cream

1 tablespoon SomerSweet

1 tablespoon instant decaf espresso powder, dissolved in 1 tablespoon hot water, or 1 tablespoon brewed decaf espresso

1 tablespoon unsweetened cocoa

SOMERSWEET SUBSTITUTIONS
saccharin: 2½ teaspoons
sugar: ¼ cup plus
  1 tablespoon

LEVEL TWO

DESSERTS

ASIAN NAPOLEONS

LEVEL TWO / Makes 4 napoleons

This is a beautiful recipe to make for company. I use crispy, deep-fried wontons to form the layers of this spectacular napoleon. Look for packages of fresh wontons in the produce section of your grocery store.

In a small saucepan heat oil to 375°. If you don't have a thermometer to test your oil, use a small piece of wonton as a test. If the oil bubbles immediately when the wonton is added, it's hot enough.

Place a cookie sheet lined with paper towels on the counter next to the stove. Using tongs, place wontons one at a time into the hot oil. Turn every few seconds, until the wonton starts to lightly brown. Wontons will continue to darken even when removed from oil. Be careful; they can burn very quickly.

Remove each wonton from the oil and place on the paper towels. Then drain and blot excess oil.

Place 8 cooled wontons on a work surface. Spread or pipe about 1 tablespoon of custard on each wonton. Layer sliced strawberries on top of the custard. Dollop another tablespoon of custard on top of the strawberries.

Take 4 of the wontons layered with custard and berries and stack them on top of the other four. (Starting from the bottom, you should have wonton, custard, strawberries, custard, wonton, custard, strawberries, custard.) Then top each stack with the remaining 4 wontons to finish the napoleons.

Sprinkle each napoleon with the sweetened cinnamon and serve immediately.

Vegetable oil for frying
12 wonton skins
1 cup Vanilla Custard
  (page 37)
8–10 large strawberries,
  hulled and thinly sliced
1 tablespoon cinnamon
  mixed with 1½ teaspoons
  SomerSweet

SOMERSWEET SUBSTITUTIONS
saccharin: 1 teaspoon
sugar: 1 tablespoon

LEMON CURD IN PHYLLO CUPS

LEVEL TWO / Serves 6

These phyllo cups are perfect for dessert at a spring lunch. *Phyllo* (FEE-loh) is the Greek word for "leaf." In culinary terms, it refers to the tissue-thin layers of pastry dough used in many Greek desserts. It is very similar to strudel dough and now can be purchased in most supermarkets. Look for it in a long box in the freezer case. To make these cups, you will need a muffin tin.

Preheat oven to 350°.

The trick to working with phyllo dough is to keep it moist. Defrost the amount you need and keep the rest of the sheets frozen. Have a damp dish towel ready to cover the phyllo dough so that it does not dry out while you are working with it.

Each phyllo cup is made from six squares of phyllo layered on top of one another. To cut each phyllo sheet into six equal squares, cut along the length of the sheet to get three equal long strips of phyllo. Then cut the three strips to form six squares.

Press each square of phyllo dough into a buttered muffin cup. Brush each phyllo cup with melted butter, then layer another square of phyllo. Continue until all 6 layers are placed in each muffin cup.

Bake for 9–10 minutes or until the pastry is lightly browned. Carefully remove the cups from the muffin tin and cool on a wire rack.

To serve, spoon chilled Lemon Curd into each cup. Top with berries and a dollop of Perfectly Whipped Cream.

LEMON CURD

Level One / Makes 2 cups

Beat the egg yolks with SomerSweet in a stainless steel bowl until blended. Add the lemon juice. Place the bowl over a saucepan of simmering water, and stir until the mixture thickens and coats the back of a wooden spoon. Stir in the butter until smooth.

Cool to room temperature and refrigerate until needed.

---

6 sheets frozen phyllo
dough, thawed
6 tablespoons unsalted
butter, melted
1 recipe Lemon Curd (below)
1 pint fresh raspberries
Perfectly Whipped Cream
(page 15)

LEMON CURD
5 large egg yolks
3 tablespoons SomerSweet
2/3 cup fresh lemon juice
(about 5–6 squeezed
lemons)
4 tablespoons (½ stick)
diced unsalted butter at
room temperature

SOMERSWEET SUBSTITUTIONS
saccharin: 2 tablespoons
sugar: 1 cup

CHOCOLATE BUNDT CAKE

LEVEL TWO / Serves 12–16

This light, airy cake gives you all the satisfaction of good ol' chocolate cake without all the sugar bingeing! Unlike my gooey chocolate cakes made with mostly Pro/Fats, this one has more carbs. It's made with whole wheat flour, unsweetened chocolate, and SomerSweet. Delightful for Level Two.

Preheat oven to 350°.

Grease a 10-inch nonstick Bundt pan with butter. (You can also use an angel food cake or tube pan.) Take 2 tablespoons of the flour and coat the pan.

Mix together the remaining flour, SomerSweet, cocoa powder, baking powder, baking soda, and salt in a bowl.

Sift the dry ingredients into a large mixing bowl.

In a separate bowl beat the egg whites until frothy. To the egg whites, add the mayonnaise, vanilla, cream, water, and coffee. Whisk until well blended.

Pour the wet mixture into the dry ingredients and stir thoroughly to form a batter. Scrape the batter into the Bundt pan, tapping to distribute evenly.

Bake in the center of the oven for 20–30 minutes or until a toothpick inserted into the center of the cake comes out clean.

Cool on a wire rack for 20 minutes. Invert cake and cool completely. Before serving, drizzle with Chocolate Glaze.

CHOCOLATE GLAZE

Almost Level One / Makes enough for one Bundt cake

Heat the cream and chocolate together in a heavy-bottomed saucepan over low heat until melted. Whisk in the remaining ingredients until well blended. Mixture will thicken as it cools. Refrigerate until needed.

CAKE

Unsalted butter for the pan
2 cups whole wheat flour
½ cup plus 2 teaspoons SomerSweet
1 cup unsweetened cocoa powder
1 teaspoon baking powder
1½ teaspoons baking soda
1 teaspoon salt
4 large egg whites
1 cup mayonnaise
1 tablespoon vanilla
½ cup heavy cream
½ cup water
2 tablespoons instant decaf coffee dissolved in 1 cup boiling water
1 recipe Chocolate Glaze (below)

SOMERSWEET SUBSTITUTIONS
saccharin: ¼ cup
sugar: 1¾ cups

CHOCOLATE GLAZE

1½ cups heavy cream
2 ounces (2 squares) unsweetened chocolate
1 tablespoon SomerSweet
1 tablespoon vanilla
¼ cup unsweetened cocoa
Generous pinch baking soda

SOMERSWEET SUBSTITUTIONS
saccharin: 2 teaspoons
sugar: ¼ cup

WHITE CHOCOLATE TORTA

LEVEL TWO / Serves 10–12

Torta is the Italian word for tart, pie, or cake. This one is made with white chocolate and it's very rich. Look for white chocolate that's made with real cocoa butter for the best flavor. Remember, white chocolate has a lot of sugar in it, so enjoy a small slice of this rich and delicious torta.

Preheat oven to 350°.

Line the bottom of a 6-inch springform pan with two layers of waxed paper. Butter the sides and the waxed paper.

Place the softened butter in a mixing bowl and beat on high speed with an electric mixer until light and fluffy.

Add the eggs one at a time and continue beating until combined. The mixture will not be smooth at this stage.

Add the SomerSweet and vanilla. Beat for another 30 seconds.

In a double boiler on very low heat melt the white chocolate, stirring constantly until smooth.

Slowly pour the melted chocolate into the egg mixture, stirring consistently until a thick batter forms.

Pour the batter into the prepared pan and bake for 25 minutes.

Cool to room temperature and refrigerate for at least 3 hours or overnight.

Run a warm knife around the edge of the torta to loosen it before releasing the springform.

Butter for the pan
4 ounces (½ stick) butter, softened
6 large eggs at room temperature
1½ teaspoons SomerSweet
1 teaspoon vanilla
1 pound (16 ounces) white chocolate, roughly chopped, or chips

SOMERSWEET SUBSTITUTIONS
saccharin: ¾ teaspoon
sugar: 1 tablespoon

WILD MOUNTAIN BLUEBERRY PIE

LEVEL TWO / Serves 8

There's something about a freshly baked pie that warms your soul. This one is made with fresh or frozen blueberries, but you can substitute any type of berries you want.

Preheat oven to 400°.

In a medium mixing bowl gently mix together the berries, butter, and Somer-Sweet.

Sift the cornstarch over the berries and let stand 15 minutes.

Grease a pie pan and line it with half of the rolled-out dough. Fill with the berries.

Using a cookie cutter, cut out shapes with the remaining rolled dough and place the shapes over the berries.

(For a glossy crust, beat one egg with a teaspoon of water and apply to the dough with a pastry brush before baking.)

Bake for 40–45 minutes or until crust is dark golden brown.

Cool for a few hours before cutting and serving.

7 cups blueberries (or mixed berries), fresh or frozen
3 tablespoons unsalted butter, melted
2 tablespoons SomerSweet
2 tablespoons cornstarch
2 recipes Whole Wheat Pastry Crust (page 77)

SOMERSWEET SUBSTITUTIONS
saccharin: 1 tablespoon
sugar: ½ cup, depending on the sweetness of the berries

STRAWBERRY CUSTARD TART
with WHOLE WHEAT PASTRY CRUST
LEVEL TWO / Serves 8

This is such a happy tart. I love the ripe, red berries and the smooth custard with the sweet crust.

WHOLE WHEAT PASTRY CRUST

Preheat oven to 400°. Butter and flour a 9-inch tart or pie pan.

Combine the flour and SomerSweet in a mixing bowl. Add the softened butter and work together with your fingertips or a pastry blender. Make a well in the center of the mixture (push the flour mixture to the sides of the bowl) and add the egg yolk, vanilla, and lemon juice.

Mix the wet ingredients together with your fingertips, then slowly incorporate the dry ingredients until the dough forms a ball and no longer adheres to your hands. Flatten out the ball with your hands. Wrap each disk with waxed paper and refrigerate for at least 30 minutes. Roll out the dough on a floured board.

Place the rolled dough in the greased pie or tart pan, poke the bottom of the crust with a fork in several places, and bake for 10–15 minutes, until golden brown.

CUSTARD

Combine the SomerSweet, cream, and cornstarch in a heavy-bottomed saucepan. Heat over medium heat, whisking constantly, until boiling. Lower the heat and continue to cook for about 1 minute, still whisking. Set aside to cool slightly.

Whisk the egg yolks lightly in a stainless steel bowl. Add the hot cream mixture to the egg yolks and whisk until light and frothy. Pour the mixture back into the pan and whisk gently over medium heat until smooth and thick, about 2 minutes. Remove from the heat and add the vanilla. Chill for about 2 hours.

Fill the cooled crust with the chilled custard and arrange the sliced berries in a spiral pattern.

WHOLE WHEAT PASTRY CRUST

1 cup whole wheat flour
2 tablespoons SomerSweet
6 tablespoons (¾ stick) unsalted butter, softened
1 large egg yolk
1 teaspoon vanilla
1 tablespoon fresh lemon juice

SOMERSWEET SUBSTITUTIONS
saccharin: 3 teaspoons
sugar: 2 tablespoons

CUSTARD

1 tablespoon plus 1 teaspoon SomerSweet
2½ cups heavy cream
¼ cup cornstarch
4 large egg yolks
½ teaspoon vanilla
1 pint fresh strawberries, sliced

SOMERSWEET SUBSTITUTIONS
saccharin: 3 teaspoons
sugar: ½ cup

Index

About the Author

SUZANNE SOMERS is the author of ten books, including the *New York Times* bestsellers *Keeping Secrets; Eat Great, Lose Weight; Get Skinny On Fabulous Food;* and *Eat, Cheat, and Melt the Fat Away.* The former star of the hit television programs *Three's Company* and *Step by Step,* Suzanne is one of the most respected and trusted brand names in the world, representing cosmetics and skin care products, apparel, jewelry, a computerized facial fitness system, fitness products, and a dessert line called SomerSweet. Please visit Suzanne at SuzanneSomers.com.